THE USBORNE BOOK OF
DINOSAURS

Susan Mayes

Designed by Steve Page

Illustrated by Luis Rey

Additional illustrations by Stuart Trotter

Consultant: Mike Howgate M.Sc.

Contents

Before the dinosaurs

Hundreds of millions of years ago, there were no land animals. There were only water creatures. Some of these began to crawl onto dry land.

Their bodies changed bit by bit. They got better and better at living out of water. Millions of years later they had changed into land animals.

Crawling fish

The fish in this picture could crawl. When the water it lived in started to dry up, it crawled onto land to look for a new pool.

Eusthenopteron
use-then-opter-ron

Names

Under each animal's name there is *italic* writing. This shows you how to say each part of the name.

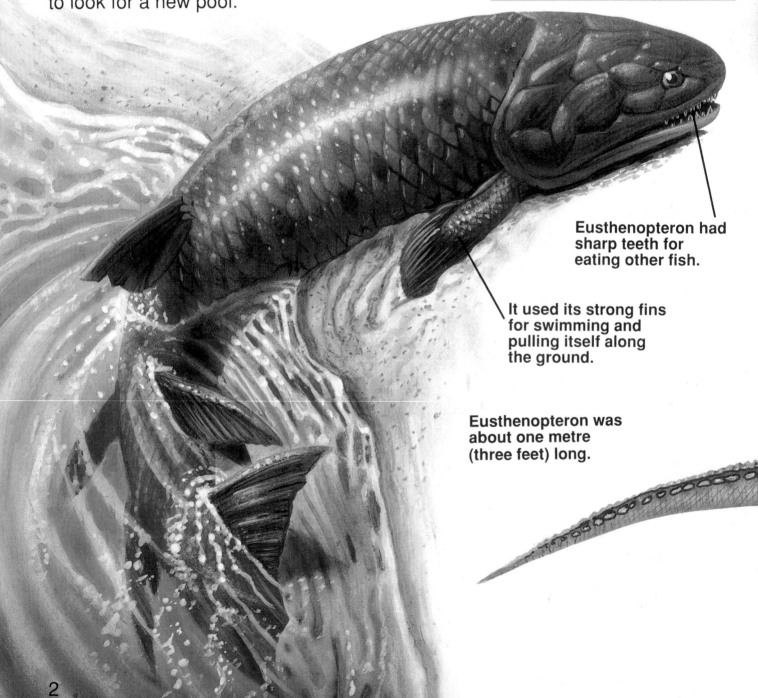

Eusthenopteron had sharp teeth for eating other fish.

It used its strong fins for swimming and pulling itself along the ground.

Eusthenopteron was about one metre (three feet) long.

2

Amphibians

Later, there were animals with legs. They lived on land, but they laid their eggs in water, like fish. They were called amphibians.

Ichthyostega
ik-thee-os-teega

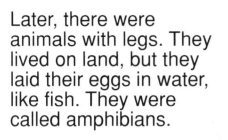

Ichthyostega had smooth, soft skin and a fishy shape for swimming.

It had a tail fin, like a fish's tail.

Its eggs were covered with jelly, like frogspawn.

Its tummy probably dragged along on the ground.

Amphibians had legs to make walking easier.

Reptiles

Some amphibians kept changing very slowly. They grew stronger, straighter legs and they lost their fishy tail fin.

They changed more and more, until they became new animals called reptiles. Reptiles lived on land and laid their eggs there, too. Dinosaurs were reptiles.

Euparkeria
you-park-eary-a

This reptile lived just before the dinosaurs.

Euparkeria walked on all four legs, but it probably ran on its strong back legs, like this.

Its skin was dry and scaly.

Its eggs had shells, so they did not dry up in the sun.

3

The first dinosaurs

Dinosaurs lived at different times and in different places. They even ate different things and they were all shapes and sizes. Here are some of the first ones.

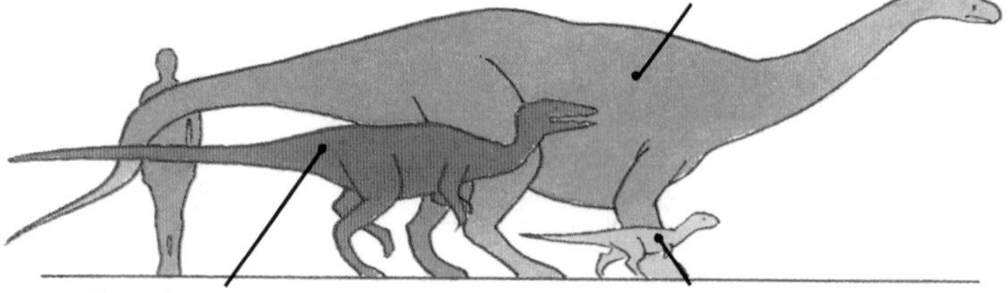

Coelophysis

see-low-fie-sis

Animals which eat other creatures are called meat-eaters, or carnivores.

Coelophysis was one of the first meat-eating dinosaurs. It lived about 215 million years ago.

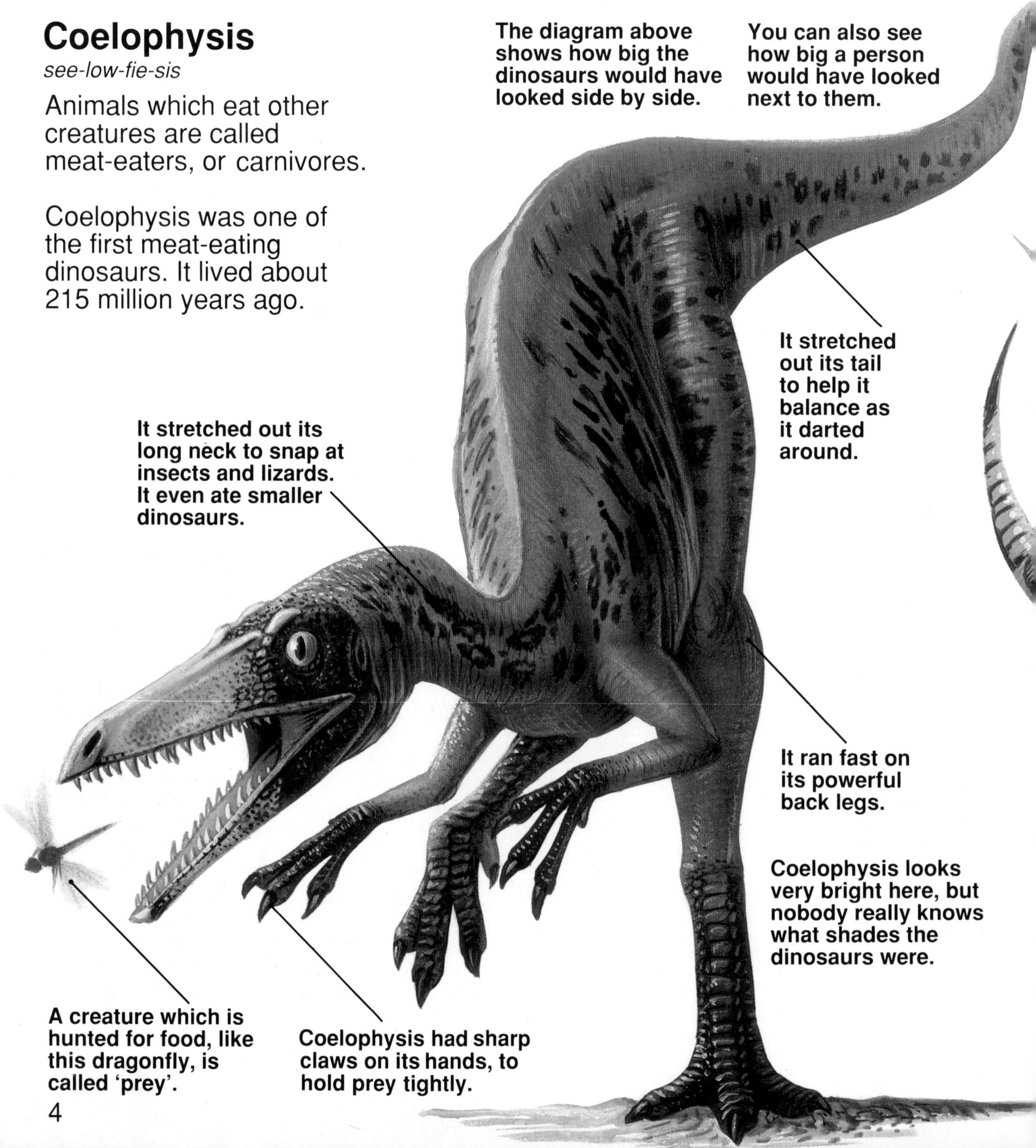

Plateosaurus

Coelophysis

Heterodontosaurus

The diagram above shows how big the dinosaurs would have looked side by side.

You can also see how big a person would have looked next to them.

It stretched out its tail to help it balance as it darted around.

It stretched out its long neck to snap at insects and lizards. It even ate smaller dinosaurs.

It ran fast on its powerful back legs.

Coelophysis looks very bright here, but nobody really knows what shades the dinosaurs were.

A creature which is hunted for food, like this dragonfly, is called 'prey'.

Coelophysis had sharp claws on its hands, to hold prey tightly.

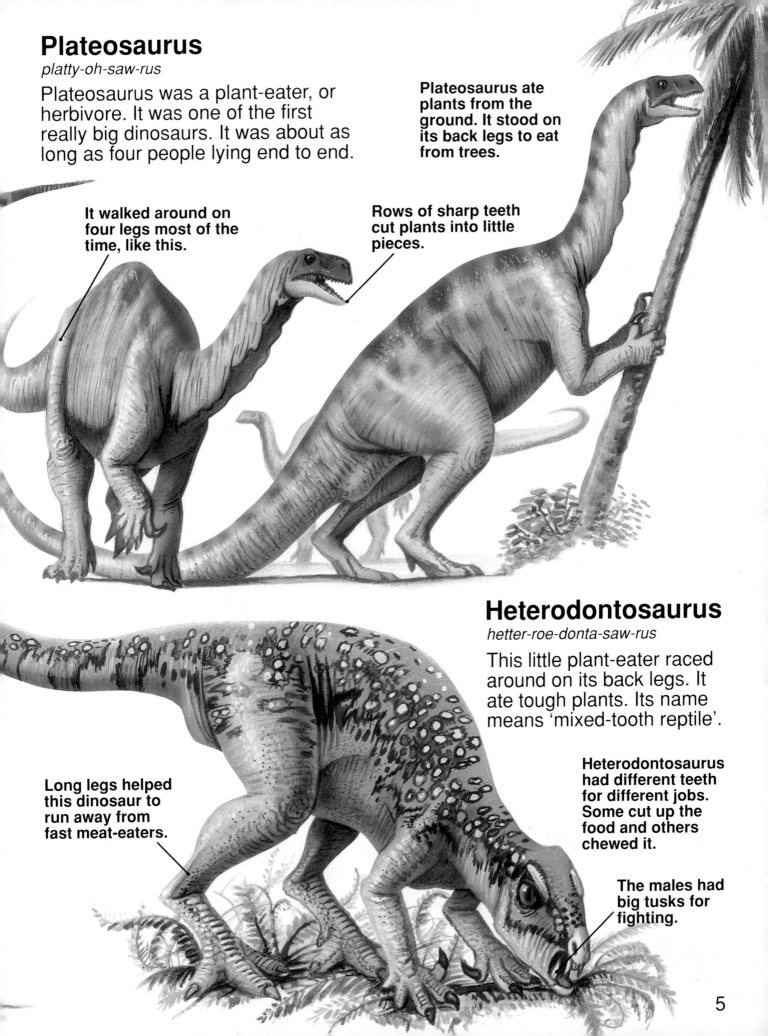

Plateosaurus

platty-oh-saw-rus

Plateosaurus was a plant-eater, or herbivore. It was one of the first really big dinosaurs. It was about as long as four people lying end to end.

Plateosaurus ate plants from the ground. It stood on its back legs to eat from trees.

It walked around on four legs most of the time, like this.

Rows of sharp teeth cut plants into little pieces.

Heterodontosaurus

hetter-roe-donta-saw-rus

This little plant-eater raced around on its back legs. It ate tough plants. Its name means 'mixed-tooth reptile'.

Heterodontosaurus had different teeth for different jobs. Some cut up the food and others chewed it.

Long legs helped this dinosaur to run away from fast meat-eaters.

The males had big tusks for fighting.

5

Dinosaur giants

The biggest land animals that ever lived were the sauropod dinosaurs. They were plant-eaters with very long necks and tails.

Diplodocus

dip-low-doe-kus

Diplodocus was longer than two buses put end to end.

Diplodocus

The bones in its back and neck were hollow. They were light and strong.

Big, strong legs carried this huge creature. It was almost as heavy as two elephants.

This long neck helped Diplodocus reach up to the treetops, to eat high leaves.

These dinosaurs walked around on four legs, but they sometimes stood on their back legs to feed.

The end of its tail was very thin. It could be used to whip enemies.

This sharp thumb claw was probably used for fighting.

Scientists think sauropods marched in groups called herds, like elephants do.

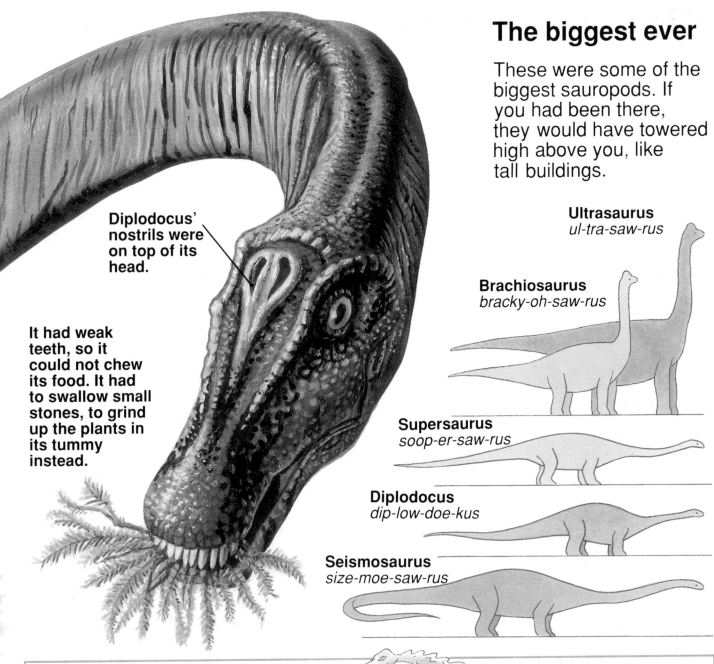

Diplodocus' nostrils were on top of its head.

It had weak teeth, so it could not chew its food. It had to swallow small stones, to grind up the plants in its tummy instead.

The biggest ever

These were some of the biggest sauropods. If you had been there, they would have towered high above you, like tall buildings.

Ultrasaurus
ul-tra-saw-rus

Brachiosaurus
bracky-oh-saw-rus

Supersaurus
soop-er-saw-rus

Diplodocus
dip-low-doe-kus

Seismosaurus
size-moe-saw-rus

Discovering dinosaurs

When some dinosaurs died, their bones were buried. Over thousands of years they turned to stone. These stony remains are called fossils.

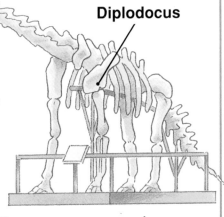

Diplodocus

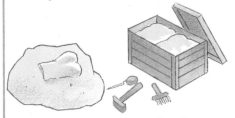

When scientists find dinosaur fossils, they dig them up, wrap them and pack them in boxes.

Later, they try to fit the fossils together, to find out what the dinosaur looked like.

Some museums have dinosaur skeletons. You can go and see them for yourself.

Big hunters

The meat-eating dinosaurs you can see here were called carnosaurs. They were enormous hunters with short arms and big heads. They walked on powerful back legs.

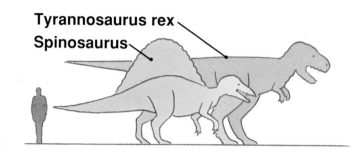

Tyrannosaurus rex
Spinosaurus

Tyrannosaurus rex

tie-ranna-saw-rus rex

Tyrannosaurus rex was one of the biggest carnosaurs.

What it ate

Tyrannosaurus rex ate plant-eating dinosaurs. Here are some of them.

Parasaurolophus
parra-saw-rollo-fus

Euoplocephalus
you-oh-ploe-seffa-lus

Triceratops
try-serra-tops

It also ate dead dinosaurs that it found.

It had big, strong leg muscles.

It was so heavy, it could only run fast for a little while. It probably waited for its prey and made a quick attack.

Its big, wide feet had curved claws.

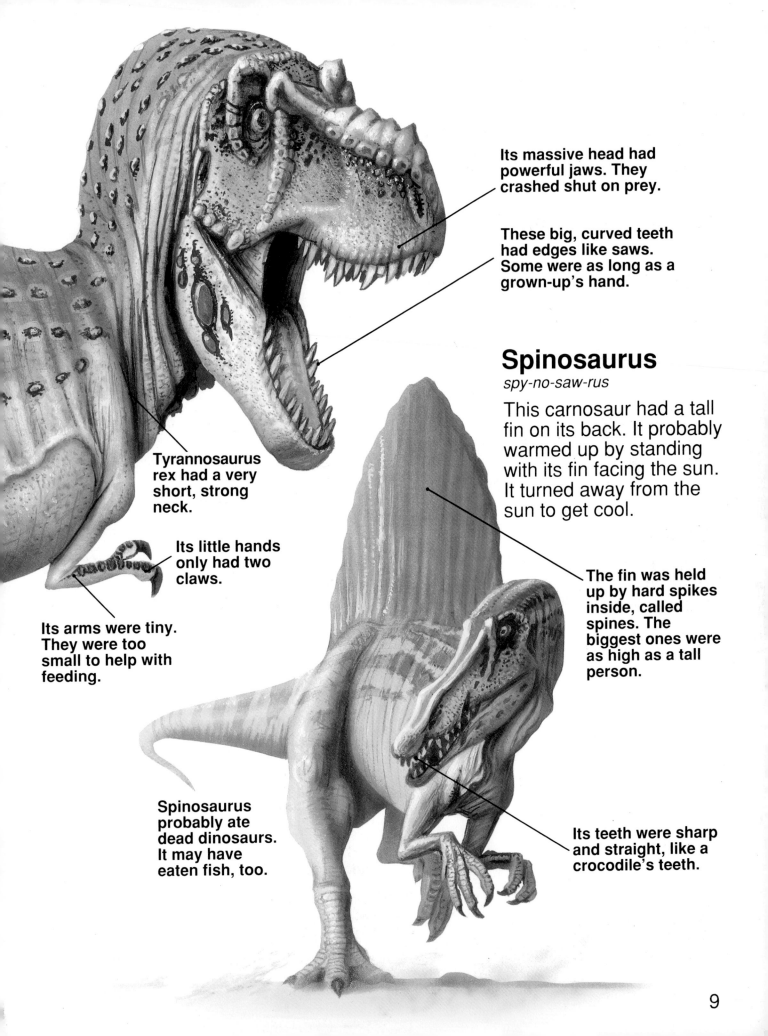

Its massive head had powerful jaws. They crashed shut on prey.

These big, curved teeth had edges like saws. Some were as long as a grown-up's hand.

Tyrannosaurus rex had a very short, strong neck.

Its little hands only had two claws.

Its arms were tiny. They were too small to help with feeding.

Spinosaurus
spy-no-saw-rus

This carnosaur had a tall fin on its back. It probably warmed up by standing with its fin facing the sun. It turned away from the sun to get cool.

The fin was held up by hard spikes inside, called spines. The biggest ones were as high as a tall person.

Spinosaurus probably ate dead dinosaurs. It may have eaten fish, too.

Its teeth were sharp and straight, like a crocodile's teeth.

Fast and fierce

Some meat-eating dinosaurs chased their prey at high speeds. They ran and leaped using their long back legs.

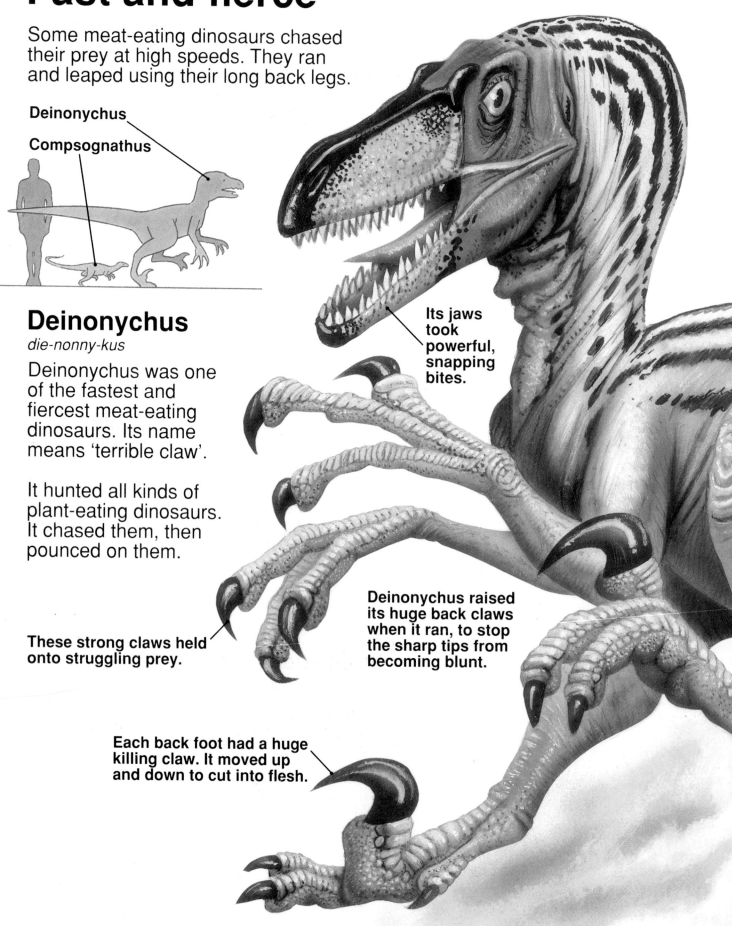

Deinonychus

Compsognathus

Deinonychus

die-nonny-kus

Deinonychus was one of the fastest and fiercest meat-eating dinosaurs. Its name means 'terrible claw'.

It hunted all kinds of plant-eating dinosaurs. It chased them, then pounced on them.

Its jaws took powerful, snapping bites.

These strong claws held onto struggling prey.

Deinonychus raised its huge back claws when it ran, to stop the sharp tips from becoming blunt.

Each back foot had a huge killing claw. It moved up and down to cut into flesh.

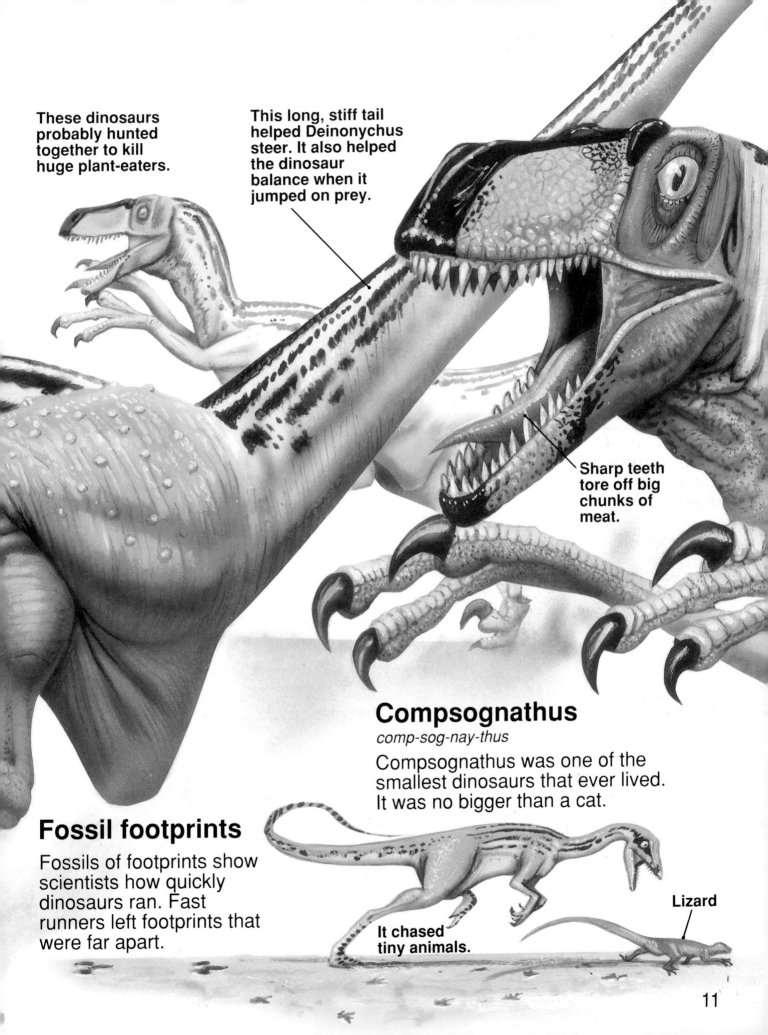

These dinosaurs probably hunted together to kill huge plant-eaters.

This long, stiff tail helped Deinonychus steer. It also helped the dinosaur balance when it jumped on prey.

Sharp teeth tore off big chunks of meat.

Compsognathus

comp-sog-nay-thus

Compsognathus was one of the smallest dinosaurs that ever lived. It was no bigger than a cat.

Fossil footprints

Fossils of footprints show scientists how quickly dinosaurs ran. Fast runners left footprints that were far apart.

It chased tiny animals.

Lizard

Runaway dinosaurs

Some dinosaurs ran fast to escape from danger. They raced away from fierce, meat-eating dinosaurs.

Struthiomimus
Hypsilophodon
Lesothosaurus

Struthiomimus

stroo-thee-oh-my-mus

Struthiomimus was one kind of ostrich dinosaur. It was a very fast runner.

Ostrich dinosaurs got their name because they were the same sort of shape as ostriches today.

Struthiomimus probably ran as fast as 45 kilometres (28 miles) an hour.

This long, bony tail stretched out behind. It helped the dinosaur balance as it ran.

Its back legs were long and powerful. They took big strides. They probably kicked enemies, too.

Big, clawed feet were good for running very fast.

Its front legs were too short to run on.

Other fast runners

Lesothosaurus and Hypsilophodon were speedy plant-eaters. They lived a long time before Struthiomimus. They were much smaller and lighter than Struthiomimus, but they ran almost as fast.

Lesothosaurus
less-oh-toe-saw-rus

Hypsilophodon
hips-ill-offa-don

Struthiomimus bent its long neck to look out for danger.

Big eyes were good for spotting enemies.

The mouth was like a bird's beak. It did not have any teeth.

Struthiomimus ate plants. It may have eaten insects and tiny creatures too, and even other dinosaurs' eggs.

These long, thin claws probably gripped food tightly.

Dinosaur armour

The dinosaurs you can see here were peaceful plant-eaters. They had 'armour' to help protect them from all the dangerous meat-eaters which lived at the same time.

Euoplocephalus

Scelidosaurus

Polacanthus

Big spikes and plates made good armour.

Euoplocephalus

you-oh-plo-seffa-lus

Euoplocephalus had leathery skin. Lots of bony lumps and bumps grew out of it.

Thick bone covered its head, like a helmet.

Scelidosaurus

skell-idda-saw-rus

This is the oldest armoured dinosaur which scientists know about.

Its tail was long and strong.

Its bumpy armour grew in rows.

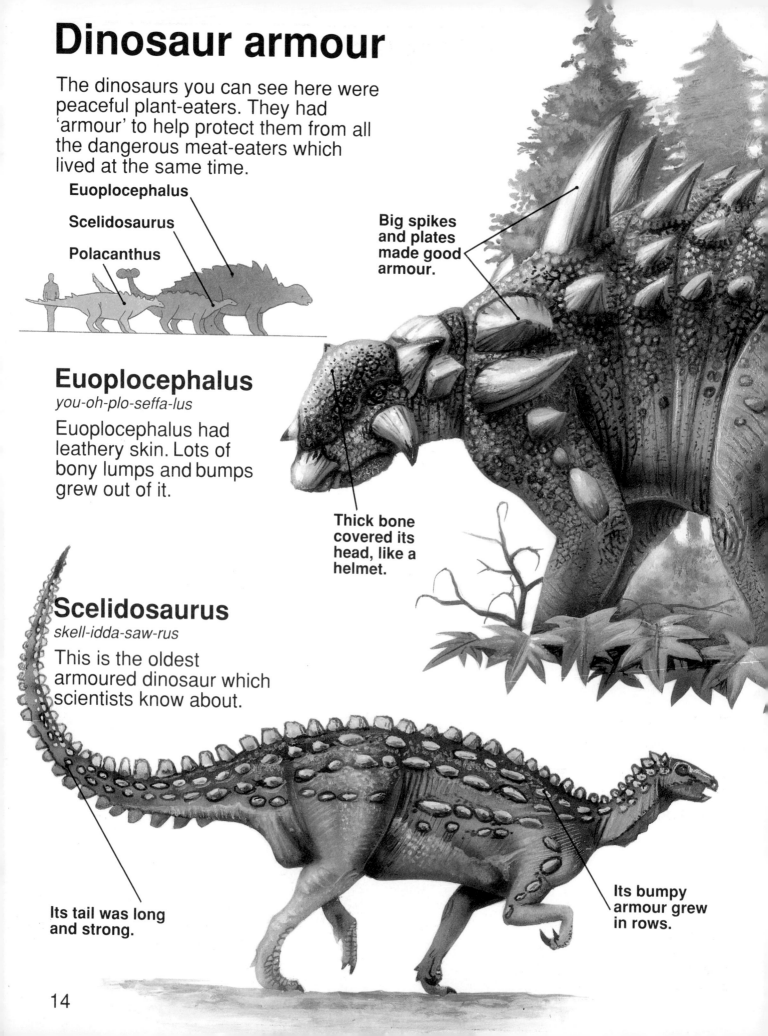

Euoplocephalus could move around easily because its skin could bend between these armoured bands.

Fighting back

If an enemy came near, Euoplocephalus swung its tail-club to one side.

Then it swung it back again to hit the dinosaur with an almighty thump.

Chunks of bone grew at the end of its tail. They made a dangerous club.

There was no armour underneath.

Powerful muscles swung its tail from side to side.

Polacanthus
polla-can-thus

This dinosaur had armour with lots of long spikes to keep it safe.

This patch of skin was extra strong, like a shield.

Armoured dinosaurs probably crouched down when enemies came near.

Its soft tummy was safe under here.

Horned dinosaurs

The ceratopian dinosaurs had horns on their heads and a bony frill around their necks. They were heavy, plant-eating dinosaurs.

Triceratops

try-serra-tops

Triceratops was the biggest ceratopian. Its name means 'three-horned face'.

Triceratops

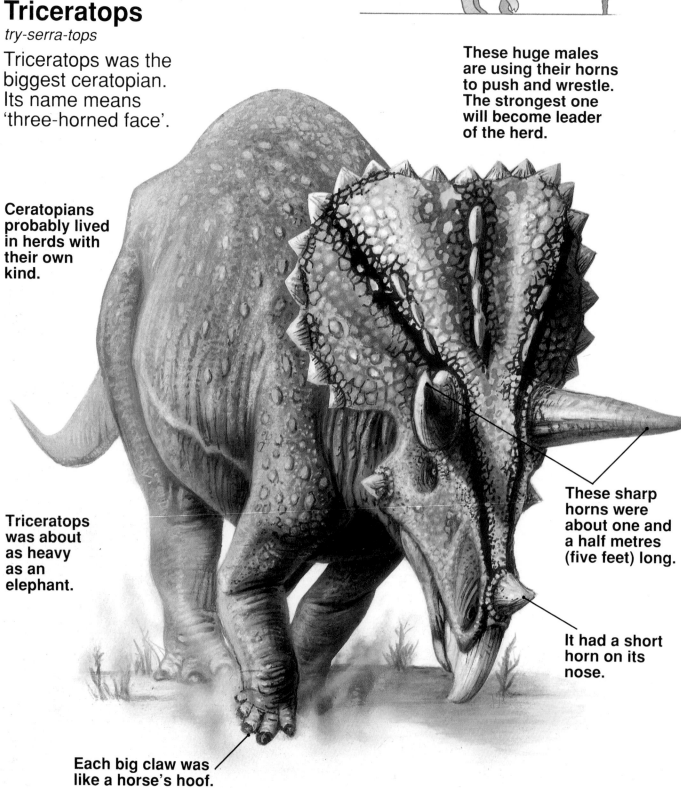

These huge males are using their horns to push and wrestle. The strongest one will become leader of the herd.

Ceratopians probably lived in herds with their own kind.

Triceratops was about as heavy as an elephant.

These sharp horns were about one and a half metres (five feet) long.

It had a short horn on its nose.

Each big claw was like a horse's hoof.

Different shapes and sizes

Here are some other kinds of ceratopian dinosaurs. Their horns and neck frills are all different shapes and sizes.

Styracosaurus
sty-rack-oh-saw-rus

Chasmosaurus
kaz-moe-saw-rus

Protoceratops
pro-toe-serra-tops

Centrosaurus
sent-roe-saw-rus

Torosaurus
torro-saw-rus

This frill was made of bone and covered with skin. It protected the neck, like a shield.

Small pieces of bone stuck out around the edge of the frill.

All ceratopians had a hooked beak, like a parrot's. It chopped through the tough plants which they ate.

Triceratops also put its head down like this to charge at meat-eating enemies. It must have looked very frightening.

Stegosaurs

The stegosaurs were plant-eaters with tall, bony plates on their backs and sharp spikes on their tails.

Stegosaurus

Kentrosaurus

These are Stegosaurus' plates. They were buried in its thick skin.

Stegosaurus

stegga-saw-rus

Stegosaurus was the biggest stegosaur. It was almost as long as a bus.

It had a beak at the end of its snout.

Its little head had a tiny brain about the size of a walnut.

Stegosaurus ate plants which grew low down. It must have needed lots of food because it was so big.

Cycad

Fern

Its back legs were longer than the front ones.

Plants probably stayed in its tummy for three or four days, until all their goodness came out.

Kentrosaurus
kent-roe-saw-rus

Kentrosaurus was one of Stegosaurus' smaller relatives. Its name means 'prickly reptile'.

If Stegosaurus was cold, it may have stood with its plates facing the sun, to help it get warm.

It had big spikes all the way down its tail.

Its plates were a different shape from Stegosaurus' plates.

It could swing its tail to stab enemies with these sharp spikes.

Stegosaurus was a slow mover. Its big body was not made for moving quickly.

Kentrosaurus had a long spike on each side of its body, to help guard it from danger.

Stegosaurus' plates

At first, scientists thought Stegosaurus' plates lay flat, like this.

Some scientists thought the plates were side by side, in pairs.

Now, many people think the plates were in two uneven rows, like this.

Hadrosaurs

Hadrosaurs were plant-eaters with oddly shaped heads. Some of them had big, hollow crests on top. Others had bony lumps and bumps.

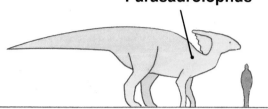

Parasaurolophus

Parasaurolophus

parra-saw-rollo-fus

Parasaurolophus had an amazing crest. It was made of curved, hollow bone and was very long.

Parasaurolophus probably made noises by blowing air through its crest. It made loud hoots to call a mate or scare enemies.

The crest began at its nostrils.

This is a male. Females had smaller crests.

The skull

Parasaurolophus' skull looked like this.

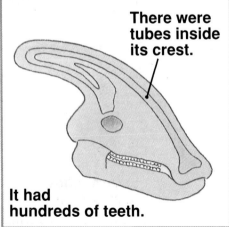

There were tubes inside its crest.

It had hundreds of teeth.

This is a female.

Hadrosaurs were also called 'duckbills' because their mouths were flat at the end, like a duck's beak.

These dinosaurs could see, hear and smell very well. They looked, listened and smelled for danger.

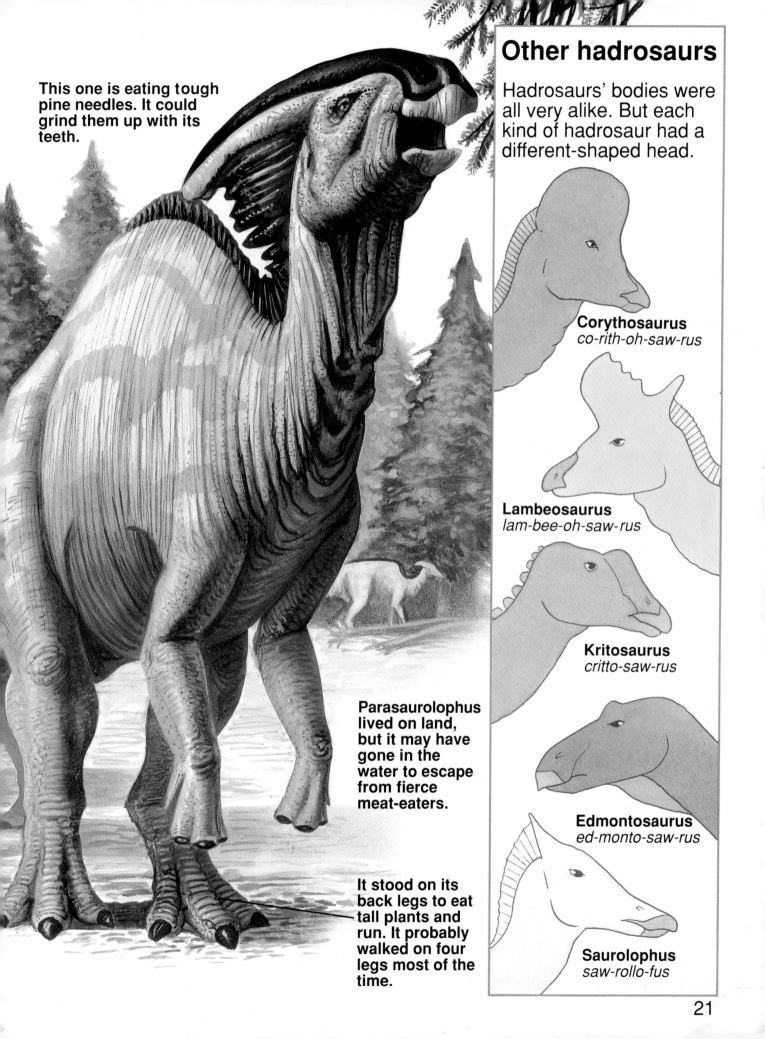

This one is eating tough pine needles. It could grind them up with its teeth.

Hadrosaurs' bodies were all very alike. But each kind of hadrosaur had a different-shaped head.

Corythosaurus
co-rith-oh-saw-rus

Lambeosaurus
lam-bee-oh-saw-rus

Kritosaurus
critto-saw-rus

Edmontosaurus
ed-monto-saw-rus

Saurolophus
saw-rollo-fus

Parasaurolophus lived on land, but it may have gone in the water to escape from fierce meat-eaters.

It stood on its back legs to eat tall plants and run. It probably walked on four legs most of the time.

21

Bone-headed dinosaurs

These plant-eating dinosaurs had dome-shaped skulls made of very thick bone. They lived in herds. The males had head-butting contests, to see who was the strongest.

Pachycephalosaurus

Stegoceras

Stegoceras

stegga-serras

This was the first bone-headed dinosaur ever found. It was one of the smaller kind.

Its dome was made of solid bone.

It had a fringe of bony bumps around the back and the sides of its head.

Males probably had higher domes than females. You can see how they used them for fighting at the bottom of this page.

Its back and hips were extra strong, so they did not break when the dinosaur was head-butting.

Bone-headed dinosaurs may have lived on mountains and hills, like goats and sheep today.

Head-butting

When two males had a head-butting fight, they charged at each other with their heads down. Their hard skulls banged together.

They probably did this again and again, until the weakest dinosaur gave up. The winner became the leader of the herd.

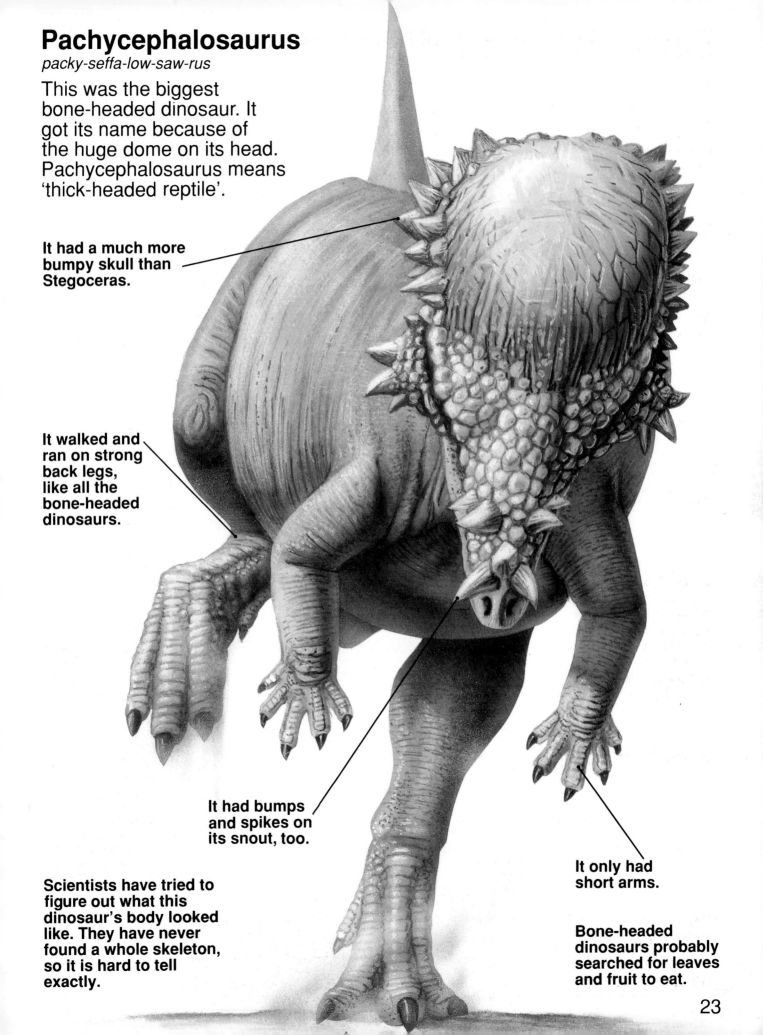

Pachycephalosaurus

packy-seffa-low-saw-rus

This was the biggest bone-headed dinosaur. It got its name because of the huge dome on its head. Pachycephalosaurus means 'thick-headed reptile'.

It had a much more bumpy skull than Stegoceras.

It walked and ran on strong back legs, like all the bone-headed dinosaurs.

It had bumps and spikes on its snout, too.

Scientists have tried to figure out what this dinosaur's body looked like. They have never found a whole skeleton, so it is hard to tell exactly.

It only had short arms.

Bone-headed dinosaurs probably searched for leaves and fruit to eat.

23

Baby dinosaurs

Baby dinosaurs hatched out of eggs laid by their mothers. Lots of fossil eggs have been found. Some belonged to a hadrosaur dinosaur called Maiasaura. This name means 'good mother lizard'.

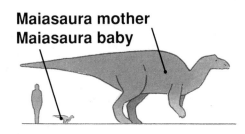

Maiasaura mother
Maiasaura baby

The sandy nests in this picture were made by Maiasaura mothers. You can see how at the bottom of this page.

Mothers made their nests close together, so there was always an adult nearby to watch for danger.

Each nest was huge. A tall person could have laid down inside.

Maiasaura
my-a-saw-ra

Leaves were piled on top. There are about 20 eggs under here.

The eggs were about as long as a grown-up's hand. Each one had a baby dinosaur curled up inside.

When a baby was ready to hatch out it broke the hard shell.

New babies were about as long as a cat.

Making a nest

The mother scraped sand into a mound and scooped out the middle.

Next, she laid her eggs carefully inside the new nest.

She piled leaves on top. As they rotted away, they kept the eggs warm.

Maiasaura babies probably stayed in their nest until they were older. Their parents brought them food.

This mother is coughing up leaves and berries which she has swallowed. This soft food was easy for the babies to eat.

Some eggs may have been eaten by egg-stealing dinosaurs or lizards.

Baby-sitting

Horned dinosaurs guarded their babies by making a circle around them. They faced enemies to scare them away.

Young sauropod dinosaurs walked in the middle of their herd. They were much safer there.

In the sea

When dinosaurs lived on the land, lots of big creatures lived in the sea. They were sea reptiles.

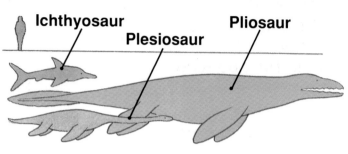

Ichthyosaur
Plesiosaur
Pliosaur

Ichthyosaurs

ick-thee-oh-sores

Ichthyosaurs were fast swimmers. They leaped out of the water as they swam. They looked a lot like dolphins today.

This tall fin helped the ichythyosaur swim steadily, without wobbling.

Ichthyosaurs did not lay eggs like other reptiles. The babies grew inside the mothers. They were born in the sea.

This smooth, curved body was good for swimming quickly.

Ichthyosaurs swam by moving this tail fin from side to side.

The flippers were used for steering.

Big eyes were good for seeing underwater.

This long snout had small spiky teeth for catching fish and other small sea creatures.

Plesiosaurs
pleesy-oh-sores

This sea reptile is a plesiosaur. It is one of the long-necked kind.

Its little head darted out to snap up fish in its sharp teeth.

It swung its long, snaky neck from side to side as it looked for food.

It rowed itself through the water with its big, flat flippers.

Its body was very big and round.

Plesiosaurs pulled themselves onto land to lay their eggs.

Pliosaurs
ply-oh-sores

Pliosaurs were a short-necked kind of plesiosaur. They were fierce and strong. They had huge heads.

Pliosaurs probably ate anything smaller than themselves. They even ate ichthyosaurs.

Strong flippers helped this pliosaur dive deep into the water to catch food.

Ammonite
amma-night

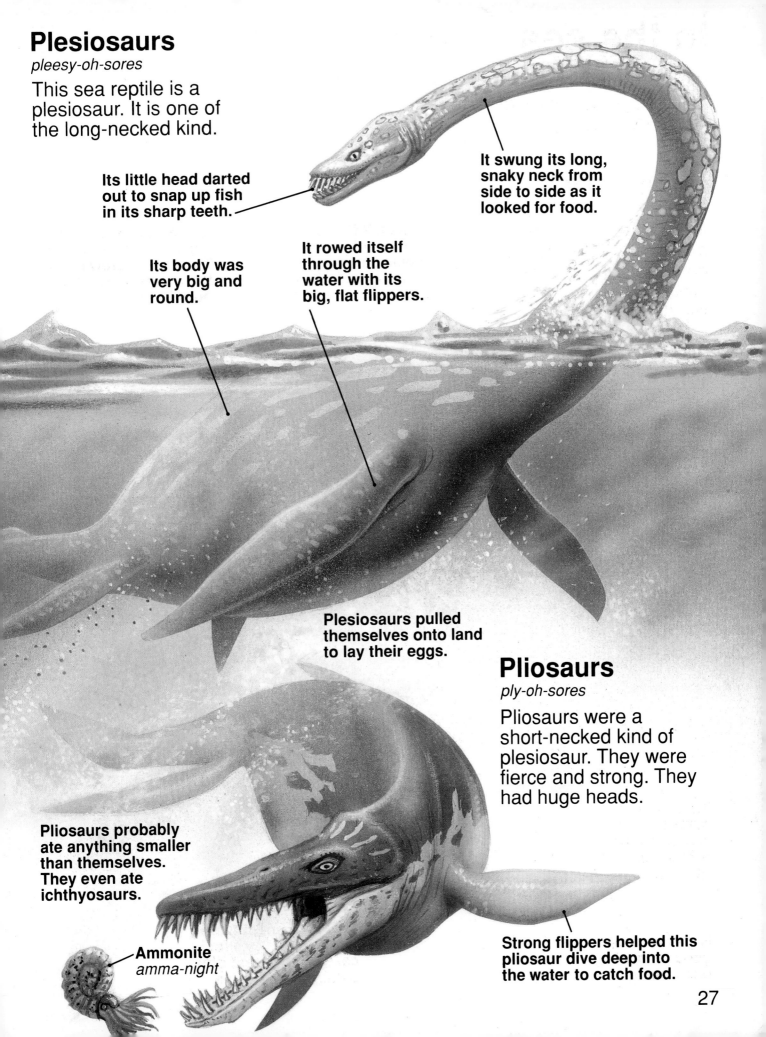

27

In the air

The pterosaurs were flying reptiles. They lived at the same time as the dinosaurs and they shared the sky with the very first kind of bird.

Pteranodon
Archaeopteryx
Rhamphorhynchus

Pteranodon

ter-ran-oh-don

This pterosaur had huge wings. It had a long, bony crest on its head.

Pteranodon's crest was made of thin bone. It was very light.

Each wing was about as long as two people lying end to end.

Some scientists think that pterosaurs had fine hair on their bodies, like this.

Pteranodon's wings were made of skin, like a bat's wings.

It did not flap its wings all the time. It glided over the sea, looking for fish to eat.

Its bones were light and hollow. This helped it to fly.

It probably had a pouch for carrying fish, like pelicans do today.

Its long beak did not have any teeth.

It only had a short, stumpy tail.

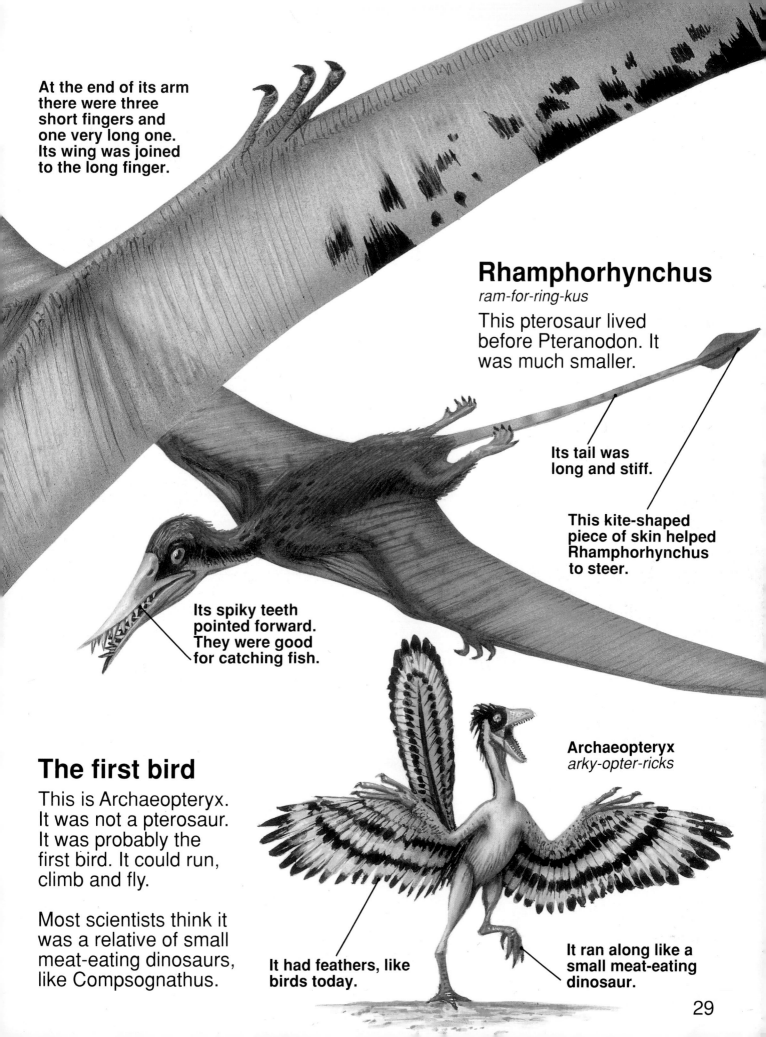

At the end of its arm there were three short fingers and one very long one. Its wing was joined to the long finger.

Rhamphorhynchus
ram-for-ring-kus

This pterosaur lived before Pteranodon. It was much smaller.

Its tail was long and stiff.

This kite-shaped piece of skin helped Rhamphorhynchus to steer.

Its spiky teeth pointed forward. They were good for catching fish.

The first bird

This is Archaeopteryx. It was not a pterosaur. It was probably the first bird. It could run, climb and fly.

Most scientists think it was a relative of small meat-eating dinosaurs, like Compsognathus.

Archaeopteryx
arky-opter-ricks

It had feathers, like birds today.

It ran along like a small meat-eating dinosaur.

29

After the dinosaurs

The dinosaurs died out about 65 million years ago. So did the sea reptiles and the pterosaurs. Nobody really knows why.

Some animals survived. Many of these were called mammals. They had fur or hair. Baby mammals grew in their mother's tummy and fed on her milk when they were born.

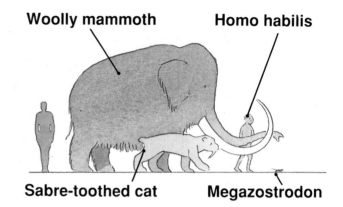

Woolly mammoth

Homo habilis

Sabre-toothed cat

Megazostrodon

Megazostrodon
megga-zost-roe-don

This tiny mammal lived at the same time as the first dinosaurs. It came out at night to hunt for insects.

Big eyes and a long nose helped it find food.

Smilodon
smill-oh-don

This fierce mammal was a kind of cat called a sabre-toothed cat. It may have hunted the big mammoth on the right.

It used its long fangs for killing.

These sharp claws held onto prey so it could not escape.

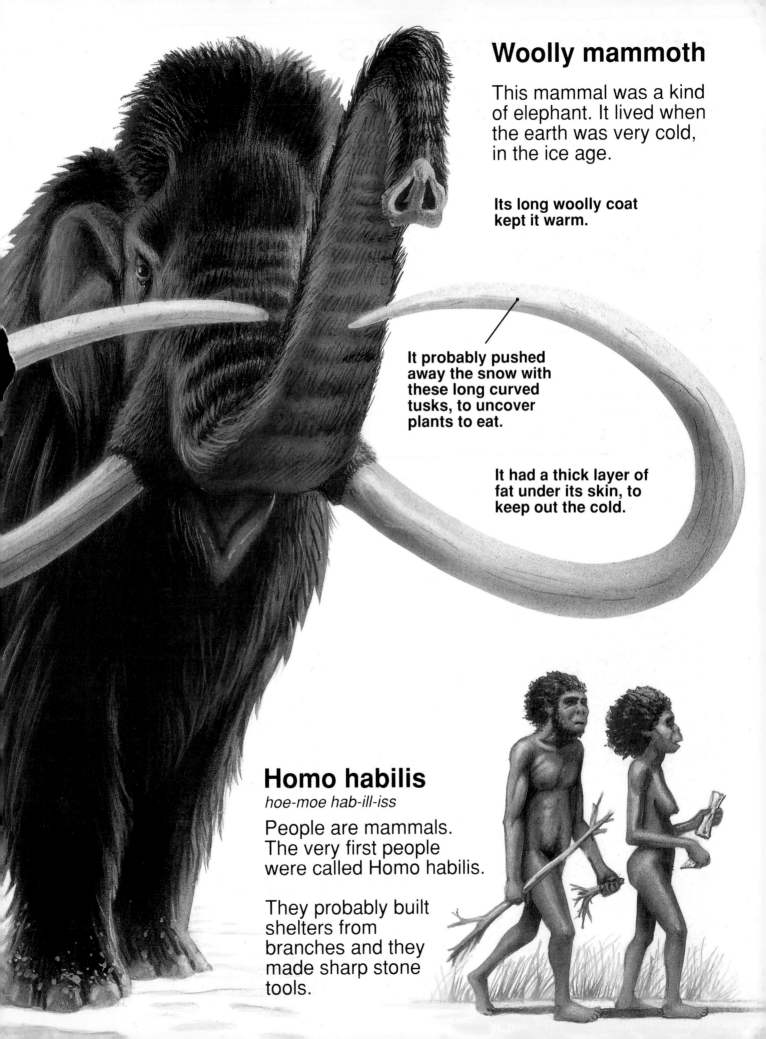

Woolly mammoth

This mammal was a kind of elephant. It lived when the earth was very cold, in the ice age.

Its long woolly coat kept it warm.

It probably pushed away the snow with these long curved tusks, to uncover plants to eat.

It had a thick layer of fat under its skin, to keep out the cold.

Homo habilis

hoe-moe hab-ill-iss

People are mammals. The very first people were called Homo habilis.

They probably built shelters from branches and they made sharp stone tools.

Index

First published in 1993 by Usborne Publishing Ltd, Usborne House, 83-85 Saffron Hill, London EC1N 8RT, England.
Universal Edition First published in America March 1993
Copyright © Usborne Publishing Ltd, 1993.
The name Usborne and the device are Trade Marks of Usborne Publishing Ltd.